Words, Words, Words

Words, Words, Words

Poems by
Jane Mary Wilde

Copyright © 2013 Jane Mary Wilde
The moral right of the author has been asserted.

Apart from any fair dealing for the purposes of research or private study, or criticism or review, as permitted under the Copyright, Designs and Patents Act 1988, this publication may only be reproduced, stored or transmitted, in any form or by any means, with the prior permission in writing of the publishers, or in the case of reprographic reproduction in accordance with the terms of licences issued by the Copyright Licensing Agency. Enquiries concerning reproduction outside those terms should be sent to the publishers.

Matador
9 Priory Business Park,
Wistow Road, Kibworth Beauchamp,
Leicestershire. LE8 0RX
Tel: (+44) 116 279 2299
Fax: (+44) 116 279 2277
Email: books@troubador.co.uk
Web: www.troubador.co.uk/matador

ISBN 9781783062119

British Library Cataloguing in Publication Data.
A catalogue record for this book is available from the British Library.

Typeset by Troubador Publishing Ltd, Leicester, UK

Matador is an imprint of Troubador Publishing Ltd

Acknowledgements

Jane Mary Wilde would like to thank Paula Jennings, Jim C. Wilson, Peter McNicol, John Glenday and Alan Hill for their help.

The 2009 edition of *Words, Words, Words,* was published by Calder Wood Press. The author would like to thank Colin Will for permission to reprint most of these poems.

288 Portobello High Street, Edinburgh, EH15 2AS

Registered charity SC 034 826

Dear reader, welcome to the C.F.P.H.'S library.

Please return this book in three weeks time as we have hundreds of people who use the library on a regular basis.

If books are returned only Months later, it prevents us from offering this much needed service for our community.

If needed, you can renew your book for another 3 weeks.

TEL: 0131 657 5680.

www.planetary-healing.org

Contents

Recipe	1
Russian Crows	2
Of the Earth	3
Bible Man	4
Sarah	5
Hagar	7
Elizabeth Rothenstein	9
Teatrum Mundi	11
Rain Dream	13
And Dog Will Have His Day	14
Mary McNaught Davis	15
Man With Handicapped Son	16
Newgrange	17
'Full Fathom Five Thy Father Lies . . .'	18
A Reminder of L'Inconnue	19
Farmer	20
A Tuscan Shepherd in Spring	21
Entertaining Angels Unawares	22
Memories of India	23
Untouchable	24
The Sais before school	25
Kanari	26
Elephant Hawk-Moth Caterpillar	27
Monkeys on a hot tin roof	29
Marbles at St. Michael's	30

Lares et Penates	31
Green Man	32
Chant for the Green Man	33
The Buddha and the Green Man	34
The Green Woman in St. Mary's Church	35
October Afternoon	36
You call us dead	37
The Doctor	38
Shadowing us	39
Bone woman	40
Exile	41
Actaeon and Artemis	42
Stratford, Midsummer	43
Fool	44
A spare and sprightly frame	45
Last term	47
Diptych	48
Bathgate Gala	49
Simon Carter	50
Ritual	51
The Marshes of Iraq	52
Krakatoan Buddha	53
Donatello's David	54
Desert	55
Honey Bee	56

Polonius: What do you read my lord?
Hamlet: Words, words, words.
Polonius: What is the matter, my lord?
Hamlet: Between who?
Polonius: I mean the matter that you read, my lord.

                Shakespeare: *Hamlet*, Act 2, Sc. 2

Recipe

Let's make a sentence.
Take each word, savour it, taste it under your tongue,
between your teeth. Sift each syllable
like autumn leaves rustled underfoot.
Look at its colour, dark or spattered with light,
edged with sea-grey. Touch it;
is it rough-textured or smooth as malachite,
ancient as fool's gold?
Does it move, will it find a place in your sentence?
Or slither and slide, defying precision?
Try to notch it in where it feels right.
Make up your mind, close with a full-stop.
And you will have silence.

Russian Crows

Westwards across winter wastes,
frozen tundra, a soaring of black wings
they come to light on milder fields
just tinged with snow;
amble like slack sentries –
children and dogs wary.

Towards evening one raucous cry
summons them to bare-branched trees
to hang like aubergines
against a bleached December sky.

A murmur of caws,
shift of wings, then silence:
until of one accord
on secret signal they rise
a multitude of clamorous wings
clashing the air,
a wild cacophony;
then quiet, and the empty
darkening sky.

Of the Earth

At first there was absence
colourless, formless, soundless.
And then the dance formed,
coloured, sounded;
light, air, earth and water
were in the dance;
sun scorched and moon refreshed
the earth.

Slime moved in the heat,
cautious slow pockets of air
seethed and simmered
into limbs, ill-defined at first,
shifting under the surface,
then thrust out by drum beats
in the dance; half-formed
eyes mouth ears
still gunged with mud.
Absence became presence.

Bible Man

I'm old. Dry-boned, slack-skinned
I skittle across scorching sand,
clamber the thorny rockland
with my flocks.
In the evening I search for the moon's ascent,
and by her impassive light, moon-wanderer,
I travel further, restless, homeless
night-long from Chaldea
to the oracle of Sechem, to Egypt
and the oaks of Mamre.
I worship the moon but at dawn she's gone.
I watch the sun spread luminous fingers
across the sky; all day he ignites the earth,
sets fire to naked feet
and burns the swollen tongue.
Rain comes, fills the wadis, showers
on seeds; eagles fan the air,
the snake angles its body towards the heat.
I worship sun and rain;
sun sets, rain stops.
There must be something out there,
some spirit in the desert
moving across the sun and moon
causing the rain the eagle and the snake.
Dare I summon it?
Dare I name its attributes, its vast infinity?
Jahweh.

Sarah

Under the Oakes of Mamre
I lie in my tent
and dream of water;
I am barren as the desert
untouched by wind and rain.

Under the Oaks of Mamre
I dream of the sojourn
in Egypt, of Abraham
and the knife-edge of our pleasure.

Under the Oaks of Mamre
I see in dream my woman
Hagar, whom I gave to Abraham
to bear him a son,
to taunt and scorn me,
and I thrust her out,
out of my pain.

Now after life-long wandering deserts
steppes and fruitful plains
after the sheep the cattle and the goats,
after Abraham, I am old
and the days of a woman are done;

Spent love corrodes me into
wasted bone and flesh,
old like a battered pot
by the dead fire.

By the Oaks of Mamre
three men come to Abraham,
and eat the new calf and drink
and wash their feet and talk –
they were the Lord God
and I eavesdropping from the tent;
God says I shall bear a son
at ninety years and he will
be God's chosen one.

And I laugh a laugh
not of scorn but wonder
and delight and disbelief,
I, years barren
and now ninety!

But the lord God is all-working,
wonderful master of wizardry
master of life and death
who can swoop and kill
or mother like a clucking hen.

"Why does she laugh?" He asks,
and I am afraid –
"Because at my age
shall I have knife-edge pleasure
with Abraham again?"

Hagar

I'm Sarah's maid,
she had me laid
by her man
old Abraham.

There rhyme and reason end.
He thrust his wrinkled leathery skin
upon my breasts,
a stench of goat and urine
under the violent desert stars.

His ancient seed took root and swelled my flesh;
I bore him Ishmael
under the violent desert sun.

He grew, a sapling
by clear water.
And I taunted Sarah who was barren,
old and useless as a battered pot
by a dead fire.

But the Lord God
gave pleasure to her and Abraham,
He filled and quickened
her ancient womb
with Isaac,
and she thrust me
and Ishmael out into the violent desert air.

Slack our water skin,
no bread,
the child under a thorn thicket,
I a bowshot distance,
not to look upon his death.

Black-tongued and lipped
he croaked his anguish
to the wheeling violent desert birds.

God heard and spoke;
"You are my son Ishmael,
I have chosen you,
a mighty race shall spring from you.
Open your eyes and see the well
and drink.
Go to the wilderness of Paran
and obey my laws."

Elizabeth Rothenstein
1905-2002
For Lucy

When you came home
no birds of prey or ill omen
hovered in the still Oxfordshire air.
The sun greeted you for the last time
this side the cosmos.
You lay in the big room
with Georgian windows
open to the garden you had tended
where you had entertained us,
made us think of life ahead
as we teetered on the edge of
adulthood.
You lay there, your skin alabaster
taut across exquisite bone,
your eyes a little open,
as a great-grand child remarked.
Another came, his hands cupfuls
of snowdrops to scatter over you,
white your shroud as the mountain snow.
In the kitchen some of us sharpened
candles for the church,
white candle flakes falling like petals
onto an old white plate.
Cups and glasses were laid out,
children ran into the room
where you lay. Then the Requiem,
the dog that had so often heard
Mass beside your wheelchair
in the same place,
now a silent witness with the rest
of us to your obsequies.
You were brought to the Church
you had tended, protected.
A grandson pondered over Paul's
Faith Hope and Love,
a rich cello sang the praise

of birds.
You left us for ashes
to be scattered across
your garden.
We returned to the house, to your room,
where Shakespeare's head
carved above the fireplace
still haunts me, as it did
when I was a child.
We talked and ate and drank,
and your spirit was there
about us; no clamorous ghost
to invade the place,
but settling on the air like blossom
falling from a tree in its own time.

Teatrum Mundi

CAT
You feed me Whiskas
stroke my fur
put bells on me
call me Puss;
you think my lives
are for this world,
to roam the rooftops,
search the night bird
and the mouse,
avoid the screech of brakes.
Make no mistake
your cat
was once Queen
upon the Thames
with sackbuts, oboes
drums and canons
praising her,
or on the Nile
her golden barge
a couch of love
for Anthony;
Khali or Parvati
floating to Krishna's flute.

DOG
My love is greatly
bounding slavering,
gambolling adoring,
my pulse beats for you.
Out of my sight
you bring world-woe.
Yet when I dream my limbs
shiver back a thousand years,
moaning of forests and the hunt –
only to wake and wag my tail.

FOX
Once you might glimpse me
red-flashing through bush,
or you could see me,
lungs bursting blood
before the hounds
tore my flesh.
Now you find me
lowering among dustbins,
my red-Reynard fur mangy,
my teeth cracked,
cubs cowering
in your gardens
and our name is vermin.
Oh where are the days
when I tricked the goose
and the lion,
frisked on a starlit night
under the swaying wind?

MAN
Go not to catch
a falling star
but money money
if you can find it
as the world gets poorer
every day.
This world is my stage,
I think feel fear ahead,
calculate, conceive
of comets,
rape the moon
count the species
under the sea.
I can catch a falling star
but where, where shall I go?
I tore the world apart
split lands apart
set folk apart from folk.
O cat dog fox
lend me your innocence!

Rain Dream

I cannot hear it rattle on the leaves,
no sound of birds, no stamp or breath from farm,
all silenced by this fall; uncanny calm
descends upon the world and seems to weave
a pall of moisture, or to hang like beads
of sweat upon the mind; no liquid balm
to ease wild thoughts, dispel the dark, disarm
the fallen angels who give no reprieve.
O stop! This is a well-worn mawkish theme;
mortality has always had its tears,
our lives are always haunted by our cry
against some god or some ancestral dream
of promise never reached; what's left is fear
of knowing what to do before we die.

And Dog Will Have His Day

Full tilt out of the hedge you came at us.
The crack
your head made as it hit our car
is like a broken sound board
in my dreams. You lay as still
as mist on new cut turf.
A friend said "Drive on. Else
the farmer will charge you. It
wasn't your fault." And we did.
Never has man or beast
been so motionless,
so suddenly cut off from teeming life
to lie inert, a lump of flesh and fur upon the road.

Mary McNaught Davis
1905-2001

A week before you died you said to me:
"I'll come and see you when it's warm".
The day you died I found myself in transit
to an island where Odysseus
roamed, where Syrinx and the Naiads
haunt the dormant pool,
flute-fingered shiver through the grass
and linger still among the Roman pines.
I hear you in the shrill cicada
and in the laughing of the gulls;
I see you in the rapid lizard
and in the timorous deer;
I feel you in the oleander bush
and in the bright warm air.

Man With Handicapped Son
On Boat From Torcello to Venice
December 2002

A painter could fix you in oil, chalk, brush –
yes, working at you, studying
your long pigtailed hair,
your empty impatient stare
as you look and do not look at your son:
A shorter pigtail, eyes emptier than yours,
a dribble on his open mouth,
he turns to us, his drowsy
"é Torcello" whispered, repeated.

A painter could not catch the words
only hint. But he would grasp your gesture,
hands outstretched
open like a lotus flower
towards the gods, frozen into a moment
of paint after ceaseless workings.
You and your son are there forever.
You move only in the eye
of the gallery globetrotter
following the fluidity of paint
within the stillness of its completion.

And words? They bend and crack
their muscles to force that moment,
can say "é Torcello"
repeat, beat, repeat, follow
your gesture from forehead to open hands,
expose your anguished impatience
but never hold you in that moment.

Newgrange
Co. Meath, Dec. 21

Winter solstice sun
gilds the rock tomb
in the earth, warms the feet
of those carrying the king
to burial.
Lay him on the smooth slab,
remove his entrails, burn them;
wash and paint his face –
woad, vermillion lips,
deep lilac eyes.

Sun sinking, push and thrust
up the darkening passage,
hustling fleet-foot
to the entrance before
the light dies.
Roll back the great stone;
silence on the way to human habitation.

Then the time of green growth,
stiff limbs moving after frosts,
fresh-killed lamb and young fish;
time to return.
Burnish the rock tomb
with torchlight, and see,
the dead king now a sapling
buds bursting from his limbs
eyes afire with stars.
Moss has settled on his skin,
streams run from his hands and feet,
birds nest in his hair;
air redolent with myrrh
and frankincense, cinnamon
and bergamot sprouting from
his living flesh.

'Full Fathom Five
Thy Father Lies...'

Wrong to say you gave us no warning,
we had three months to imagine life without you.
In bitter January we buried you
among the Poles in Gunnersbury,
where Catholics were put.
You had a good wake.

Later you were often here in dreams or thoughts.
Was something wrong? Had we buried you
in the wrong place? Should your grave have been
on some bird-spattered rock
where seas sunder and pebble-grind our ears,
or on a heady incline of the Hindu Kush?

You came once in the dark hours
a blindfold beggar; your bowl empty.
and then again – can I say for the last time? –
as naked and dead, and I found you in
some remote and vast shorn-grass place
and put you in a wheelbarrow and wheeled you
up down back forth round around
without end without respite,
until on a sudden hump of hill
I saw a fish-tank, struggled up,
you naked frail as a bird's foot
and yet a stone load weight to wheel,
and thrust towards the edge.
I tipped you in, you sank and swirled and turned.
And changed.

A Reminder of L'Inconnue Drowned in the Seine

You find me floating face-down
or hidden among undergrowth.
You lift me carefully, tenderly
into a bodybag and take me
out of the elements to lie under a roof.

You examine all my parts, take DNA;
was my end violent?
Or did I fall into oblivion
of my own volition?

A team of police and pathologists
work on my case,
worry at it like terriers,
question the sort that haunt
parks, riverbanks.

How strange that while I lived
I had no roof over my head;
no one lifted me tenderly.

Farmer

I have eleven acres and five sons.
Once, when the land bloomed,
I had more fields
for my sons to tend,
and ease me gently
into old age and death.

Always there were goats and pigs
rooting in filth by the roadside,
women crouched
over the pot on a thin flame,
swollen-bellied children
scrabbling in filth;
cows always ambled
among mad taxis, lorries, buses
spewing out fumes
into the thick still air
shattered by hoots and horns.

This was always so;
but the land, tended
as if each grain were
a precious jewel in a Rajah's crown,
sustained us on the brink of hunger.

Now my fields have shrunk
and shivered
in the heat;
the rains have not come;
as I die should I put my faith
in the wheel that turns and turns
enticing belief in –
dare I say hope in –
another better life?

A Tuscan Shepherd in Spring

He comes down stony paths across the fields
just tinged with green, his pipe now shrill now veiled
by groves of cypress and the olive, pale
in early sunlight; round his head birds reel
and plunge, his flocks shift grazing ground to steal
behind him, follow down an ancient trail
across a stream, he calling them to scale
a rocky high land with a ledge to shield
them for the night. How far this is from where
I stand and wait my turn among the crowd
at Tesco as outside the wind and rain
thrash darkness. Herbs in my trolley grew there
wild, evenings and wine were warm, the loudest
sound cicadas; I hear that song again.

Entertaining Angels Unawares

Rilke said *every angel is terrible*
not using terrible as we do
when we talk about the weather or a hat.
Nor was he thinking of fat companionable putti
lurking in the corners of great masters.

Can we conceive of the creatures
he had in mind when he asked
who would hear his cry
among the order of angels?
A rush of air thrashes the sky
with last trumpet terror;
messengers from beyond,
vast feathered beings
crushing the Word of God
out of the Prophet;
the same God's Word sharpened
to a nerve-end in a poor girl's womb.
Or angels of mercy
lead through wastelands and water,
stop the murderous sword
at Isaac's throat.

Then, they were; now, are they not
for want of our belief?
Or do they exist without us?

The whisper, not into the ear
but into a corner of the mind;
the touch, not on hand or face
but on the secret passage of the throat;
the memory, not returning to the brain
but into feet that tread some path
dimly recalled or not recalled at all
that must be followed, sometimes alone
sometimes with another.

Memories of India

Like monkeys. Bandarlog, Langur, the mind
returns to flit through sunlight, shadow, rain
that gouges nullahs out, drenches the flame
and flash of parrot wing, festers the rind
of lychees, fish-skin, fowl. Can mind define
still over years the pungent smell, the drains
and rivers, cool sluggish graves for nameless
dead; all grief erased and now forgotten grind?
But go and climb those steps above the house
and on the last step sit and concentrate
upon the distant glacial heights that tower
and shimmer in the vivid air, rousing
a child's thoughts long ago to contemplate
eternity, neglect the passing hour.

Untouchable

Day in day out
I mix dung with straw for fuel,
the stench whitening in heat.
In summer a ration of rice from over-lords,
scant payment for back-break work in fields.
My shadow cast upon their path brings ill-luck.

Winter food of rats snared in stubble
roasted over a thin flame.
Vultures circle above
day in day out
wait for my death,
not shun this meat.

The Sais before school

You were my friend.
I squatted in the dust
to watch you wash
your gleaming body
in water held in copper.
Then you ate your curry,
vegetables cooked over a brazier
in cumin, coriander, chilli,
shovelled in with fingers
and a fork my mother gave you.
Done, you licked the fork
and used it as a comb.
We went to saddle ponies,
they smelled of sweat, sweet hay and dung.

We rode to school, to Miss O'Halloran up the hill;
questions spattered round us deadly as shrapnel
from lips coated in yellow froth,
"twelve times seven seven times eight
eight times nine quick quick!"
Frozen in line some steeled themselves,
risked raising hands;
I stood mute, remembering the Sais.

Kanari

You are my pony, dunn-coloured, hot-eyed,
you take me up the Mall to school in Shimla.
The Sais bends to free a stone between his toes,
your hooves slap the dust, you bolt buck throw me,
scatter a palaver of people.
I mount again, not to school, but hurt home.
"I'll teach this brute a thing";
whip in hand, red shirt over jodhpurs
jaw a nut-cracker, the woman
slashes your velvet mouth.
Blood-flecked foam flies, sprays us.
Back in your stable I supplicate with brown sugar.
"Traitor" I hear you say,
I'll throw you again.

Elephant Hawk-Moth Caterpillar

You were huge,
your stripes like tiger not a moth,
a trunk-like body, black against a paler skin.
You had bars around your head that seemed to smile,
crinkle and glisten as you crawled about the bed,
negotiating pillow humps, mountains of sheet,
gauze mosquito net. You dined
on rhododendron leaves, magnolia, and on deodar,
roamed freely round the nursery.

They said *"we are going home"*
to somewhere overseas, cold,
shocked and racked by war now over.
The caterpillar cannot come, they said.

Packed up, the day to leave loomed
with sullen clouds, the air dense;
I went to find you, found instead the chrysalis
you had become, well-timed.

Put into a matchbox, you came with us,
train to Bombay, ship to Liverpool,
through the pitch-blue Indian Ocean
to the Red Sea, at sunset heather-hued,
the icy bay of Biscay.

You were paraded through the ship;
to Nobby Clark and Blanco White, the sailors,
to Commander King who named you James.
He said; *"A word of warning – I'm afraid he's dead."*

At first, in Bombay, even Suez
you had moved in sudden jerks.
Now, as we watched, you were so still.

Just before we docked in Liverpool
we had a ceremony on deck.
You were wrapped in cotton wool,
a plastic rose glued to your box,
Commander King said words.
We buried you at sea.

Monkeys on a hot tin roof

The monsoon is late again.
Our paws burn and blister;
we dance the cancan, bark and yowl
to ease the pain.

Is anyone at home? Silence.
Look at a chink of open window!
Send a baby down,
he'll open it and let us in.

The house is empty.
Here's a fruit bowl,
apples, mangoes, lychees, nuts,
and bits of breakfast on the table,
sugar, butter to soothe hot paws, cool milk.

Now to the bedroom
Pillows to be ripped apart,
showers of feathers,
bright jewels, not so good to eat
but well-worth hiding,
children's toys to smash.

Stop!
A door opens; the cook's mate yells at us,
drops his bag of yet more food,
carrots, ockra, onions roll out.
Grab some, bare your teeth and chatter,
then back to the roof and away with the swag.

Marbles at St. Michael's

Nothing on earth could lure her
to enter such a Catholic den of sin,
dour Heather Hurry now in charge
with Mother away,
knowing we had to go to Sunday Mass.

So off I went with Charles and Joseph,
Christian bearers from the South.
I was at ease with them, knew them well,
had visited their warm and smelly go-down
beneath our Snow-View House,
where the rabbits also stayed.
Charles let me see his pillow, lined with grease,
his name on it in grimy pink.

A Sunday walk between them down the hill,
through iron gates; monkeys idled in the courtyard,
monks greeted us.

We went to the back, where Indians sat.
Without my mother there to curb the choir
they struck up with "Ecce Sacerdos"
as priests paraded up the aisle,
and we responded "qui fecit caelum et terram"[*]

Charles and Joseph bowed and prayed,
beads clicked, bells rang,
incense swayed about the church.
Under the benches curious eyes peered at me,
small hands scattered marbles, some for me.
We played quite undisturbed, quite loud,
no fiercely whispered "quiet!" no slaps or cuffs.
The Mass sailed blissfully by.

---

[*] "Behold the Bishop", response: "who made heaven and earth"

Lares et Penates[*]

A child, I watched evening clouds massing,
made out cliffs and lakes,
forests and purple canyons,
and among them built my house.
Every night as jackals howled,
the cloud-scene changed – but always the house,
permanent, trustworthy.
Not like us, leaving and moving
to hills in summer, plains in winter.

A house of bricks and mortar now I'm old
inhabited by shadows
waiting in clusters by the door
to slide in, take over dark corners,
move silently from room to room..
They are phantoms of my past,
family, friends, a lover long dead.
I cannot hustle them away,
disperse them like smoke;
they are part of me,
intimate as skin, deep as bone.

---

[*] Roman Household Gods.

Green Man

Stiff stone-carved leaves surround my watchful face,
ghouls, fallen angels and mad beasts with wings,
harpies and haunters, everything that clings
to slime lurks with me in some shadowed place
far from the sanctuary. They give us space,
the holy ones, to draw our fangs and wring
the poison from our monstrous selves, trying
to hinder us – our powers in stone encased.
But walk among high trees far from the church
along no paths, hear withered reeds shiver
and clatter in the wind, take time away
from human hubris over me, and search
fox burrows, frozen padfall, what's winter –
hid; sense my roaming through a summer's day.

Chant for the Green Man

A felon swings
from an oak in the forest
rains wash
the filth from him
crows peck
the eyes from him
sun kindles
maggots in the sockets
to crawl into him
his clothes rot
and fall from him
the rope snaps in frost
snow covers him
foxes gnaw at him
by spring he's invaded by mosses
roots in his hair
an acorn lodged in his belly
sends out shoots
flesh and bones
change to green growth.

The Buddha and the Green Man share my garden

The Green Man lowers over unkempt flowers,
lupins past their prime,
slash of red poppies like open mouths,
marigolds splashing orange,
nasturtiums, sweet peas, thyme and rosemary.
He snarls, bites at ivy, clematis.
All this abundance grown to seed,
and yet, his forest-face remains ceramic white.

Still as a well the stone Buddha sits
under a Kilmarnock willow's shade.
His forefingers and thumbs form circles;
washed by dew rain snow
he is absorbed into the wilderness,
takes on the wild man's colour,
turning from white to green.

The Green Woman in St. Mary's Church
Pirna, Saxony, Germany, 16th c.

For Ingrid Stuhr

I stand upon a broken branch,
backed up against a tree
that rises up to join fan vaulting.

My gaze is fixed, defiant,
limbs encased in chiselled leaves
that cover all my parts,
just finger tips, teeth, hair and face seem free,
but they are frozen in the carver's wood.

The coloured leaves are cruel reminders of my past;
fertility symbol, bringer of fortune,
free-roaming mountain spirit,
solitary of woods and lakes
that lived the other side
of civil law.

Long ago they white-washed me,
afraid I might provoke believers;
now the tourist trade has made me green again.

So, put me in the church with the Green Man,
carve martens stalking birds,
and apes behind more wooden leaves;
ignore us, paint us, gawp at us;
but have you really drawn our fangs?

October Afternoon
(after Erich Fried)

Dust settles on cushions on windowsills,
makes a path for sunlight to fall on the floor,
settles on the bed, the table,
in cracks and corners of the room.

In time it becomes the room,
no longer settling but possessing,
dust on dust under dust.

In time I shall be this quiet dust
I will rest on a bed of dust
and trace the sun's path.

You call us dead

After you have witnessed
the last tumultuous hour,
the quiet cessation of breath,
or worst of all,
the bloody violent end.

There, where you cannot follow,
there where our spirits hover
in sunlight on water,
or smoke from lit driftwood on a beach,
in summer-warm lichen
like rough fur on a bell tower;
in scent of ripe apples,
taste of cloves, cinnamon, lemon;
in drifting cloud shadowing hills
we rest awhile,
or delight in speed of movement
which is neither speed nor movement,
these rooted in a time no longer ours.

Cease thought,
hold breath,
suspend the world;
and you may sense us
in a wisp of hair.

The Doctor
In Memory of Dr. Victor Sorapure* 1873-1933
For Dr. Jack Sorapure

Seen from the window of his waiting-room
autumn trees are pale, leaves dying
undress bare-boned branches.
Patients sit and wait, read "Punch",
take in the shining parquet floor,
thick curtains, the waxy cyclamens.

Called to his consulting-room
they meet a man of medium-height,
round shoulders, bulge of abdomen, smart suited,
his huge long-fingered hands
resting like thoughtful birds perched on the chair.

What could he do for the mortally sick
before the advent of the nowaday's drug?
This:

*"I can console, give opium,
injections to ease pain,
but all things will be cured in time;
today what seems useless
will be the link to cure the future.
We are lives within lives,
what we suffer now is but a part
of universal, no, do not say infinite woe.*

*Your great sickness is a piece of the repairing world.
Put your agony into this world. It will fade."*

---

* Dr. Victor Sorapure treated Katherine Mansfield.

Shadowing us

They move lightly,
observe without being observed,
follow us, gather information
like bats or silent wolves.

If the sun is behind us
they flit in front,
then just glimpsed,
vanish.

Shadowing us, do they want to know
who we are?
Are we ready to join them, or afraid?

Yes, we fear them, and with reason.
Shadows we cast do not always seem our own,
are not always two-legged with arms and head,
can have foreign limbs and segments,
a hint of wings, suggestion of fur,
of movement on all fours
with a stealth we do not have.

We try to ignore them, say they are not ours,
blame others for them, but they stay,
reminders of what lurks within;
detached from them we die.

Bone woman
After a legend of the Pueblo Indians

The forest was full of sound,
whispers, crack of branches,
shifts in the undergrowth,
lope of wolf, lion or cat.
At night the mountains and the stars
sang with insects,
fragrant water was rich with fish.

Now the forest is full of silence,
only the trees move, dying slowly.
In the undergrowth insects and frogs dwindle,
wolves leave no trace,
the lion and the cat are hunted out,
the water tainted, fish dead.

The woman looks in river beds for bones,
let's say a wolf's bones;
patiently over long, endlessly long years,
scouring, rummaging deserts, scrub, forests and plains,
she bonds together
the framework of a wolf.

She lights a fire and sings over the bones,
long song that stirs the sky, disturbs the earth.
And the bones are slowly fleshed, furred.
Fire and song flame out,
the wolf breathes.

Exile
(after Psalm 137)

The way is hard until they let us rest
on river banks where willows grow,
our grief reflected in their troubled boughs.
Unpowered
we hang our harps upon the nearest branch.
Our captors taunt and threaten us to sing
those ancient songs of our belief,
but steady as still water we refuse.
May darkness cover me if I forget
my home or lose a sense of peace,
free movement;
may my tongue cleave to my mouth
and all my actions be stillborn.
In bondage let my song remain unsung.

Actaeon and Artemis

After the hunt heat glistens on hound-skin,
sunlight tunnels through shade on water,
a pool entices Artemis and her nymphs.
Diving into brown depths
sweat and dust are washed from them.

Nearby Actaeon sights Artemis
eternal virgin, rising naked from the pool.

Water shimmers on her flesh,
his sigh of desire alerts her hounds.
She spots him slithering away
into the half-lit forest with his dogs.

If he should boast of this?
Gloat to his friends, evoke her flesh
to winos in the market place?

Antlers split his skull,
new limbs thrust through his limbs,
hooves swell from his feet
deer pelt thickens on his skin.

She has transformed him into a stag;
snaps her fingers at his hounds
who sensing prey not master
rip his throat.

Stratford, Midsummer

They are re-building the theatre.
Cranes hang their heads in limp air
as we pass, herds of us,
and the yews in New House Gardens hump together
in dark eldritch shapes.
I look down at the ground,
do not see shadows of half-timbered houses
or the chapel outline, but concentrate on
rough pavements, uneven dips, cobbles.
Is it because I now have to watch my step?
Or is cautious age drawing these stones into my soul?

Fool
Brijuni, Croatia, 2001. (Ulysses Theatre Company).

We sail in the King of France's boat
to an island where he goes to claim Cordelia,
and pull in to a narrow jetty under a plinth.
The Fool is sitting naked, high above our heads,
looking out to sea, hostile, aloof from us as we file past.

Actors and audience make their way
to a ruined fort where Lear will hold his court.
We move from roofless room to room, follow the action,
hear in Serbo-Croat "my poor fool is hang'd".

But not this Fool. Back naked on his plinth
as we go home bruised by tragedy.
Out of the play he merges
ancient kingdoms with torn lands of now;
his silence howls against a wall of deafness.

A spare and sprightly frame
In memory of "Twin", Violet Sylvia Luckham 1910-2009

You didn't lead a charmed life.
You coped, silver-tongued like Ariel,
fresh as Phoebe or Viola,
parts you played so long ago.

In the war you toured Bristol, Coventry,
were bombed out, married, had a son,
travelled the wandering players' life in digs.

When I knew you, events had simmered down;
books, beaches on Iona and on Skye,
silence – collecting stones and curious shapes
of salt-washed wood.
We sauntered among wreathes of seaweed
edging back and forwards in the swell.

Sometimes we never spoke,
sometimes we read poems aloud,
our voices muffled by the wind outside.
Candlelight and peat fire touched
the darkest corners of the room.
Last time I saw you was at Tenebrae.

Can you imagine then, the grief
you caused us all
thinking of your spare and sprightly frame encased
in coffin-wood rumbling through curtains
towards the flames?

Once more you saved me from myself,
I heard you say *"Don't be so silly darling,*
At ninety-nine my time had come."

Reading A.S. Byatt in your chair
alone at home,
you'd felt a wintry breath, heard the swish of scythe.
You looked up from your book, saw Him and said;
"Hello darling, how nice to see you.
May I just finish the chapter?"

Last Term

"Holy Mary! This ink is hot and terrible!"
wrote a monk in the margin of his manuscript
in May, Mary's month. Now May is here again,
the afternoon languid as a cat's yawn.

Rows of white-veiled girls drowse through Aves
in the chapel, incense curves and swells
in sunlight setting fire to vermillion,
blue and golden stained-glass saints.

Summer drones on.
Hormones buzz about the chapel walls
Frantic for release.
"Holy Mary! I want out!"

Diptych

ICON

Before he made me the artist retreated
into prayer and contemplation,
fasted, scrupled at sex,
meditated each tincture on his palette,
choosing lapis lazuli for heaven,
hammered gold, encrusted emerald and turquoise for my dress,
my face pale, eyes requiem-dark.
The Basilica housed me,
blackened me with candle smoke,
perfumed each fissure of my skin with incense.

THE GALLERY OWNER

She's a priceless jewel in my collection,
artist unknown;
her eyes pursue me –
seeming to question,
disquieted at these rooms
where she is housed with portraits – fur-trimmed burghers,
lush landscapes, nudes, shapes of string and tinfoil,
halved animals in formaldehyde.
All for sale.

Bathgate Gala, June 2012
In Memory of Dietrich Fischer-Dieskau

Flags plucked by the wind in cold sunlight.
The clamour of pipes, then drums;
children dressed as Dalmatians or as warriors,
some jaunty, some in prams.
A clown, blond-haired, on stilts,
and then fat Falstaff peering from his basket.

I dream of flowers and birds calling.

A winter journey in June.
Tears melt the frozen earth,
hope is a fallen leaf.
Will-o-the-Wisp hovers over firelight, candlelight.

Simon Carter
1931-2010
For Lucy

You wore subtle colours,
soft terracotta shirts,
subdued green tweeds
old but immaculate,
well-turned but casual;
a Russian hat in winter.

Your wit was sharp – once you played God
in a duologue where Jesus argued all the time.
And then your cello sang with Pablo's Birds;
your voice was silver-syllabled but firm.

Last time we met
you read a poem I'd written on The Dead.
Now you too have "shuffled off" distress,
the body's intervention;
can see the seed grow,
taste the cello note and touch the voice,
smell the curlew call
and hear the feather fall.

Ritual
For Timothy, 1941-1989

The ankle-deep brown burn ambles
over unsteady stones;
between mud banks with roots to clutch at
as we haul ourselves up
to carpets of brushwood,
brambles, bracken tendrils and malachite-green moss.
Among the trees we light a fire.

The wind drums sharp-angled forks of flame;
one by one we burn the letters.
Their ashes shrink in the wind,
fan across damp brushwood,
then dissolve.

Down the burn float
lenten roses and daffodils for remembrance.

The Marshes of Iraq

Sand, where once seeds sprang up,
marsh waters plucked at reeds:
all drained by one man's malice
and starved – cities too and children,
dissidents and unbelievers.
Eden has slipped our fingers more than once.

But hope is left and trust
in Tigris and Euphrates flooding,
then, their courses changed,
they soak parched grains
and nurse each plant,
precious as a child.

Wind thrums in grass again,
the slender-billed gull is back,
the flamingos, and a miracle,
the Basra Reed Warbler
comes home.

Krakatoan Buddha
Deep Sea World, North Queensferry

Does he remember the earth exploding,
torrents of ash spewed worldwide,
mountains, cities, temples submerged by swollen seas?
Does he remember,
as he sits in his dimlit tank,
eyes fixed by nightmare –
or resignation after the storm?

An empty gaze beyond adversity,
ears sealed against all clamour,
hands folded neatly in his lap.
Air-filtered water eases him,
fish from his island –
Bannerfish Triggerfish,
Blue-faced Angelfish,
yellow Surgeonfish
Domino Damsels
tease and stroke him
try to provoke him.

An empty gaze beyond diversity,
ears sealed against all murmur
hands folded neatly in his lap.

Donatello's David
Bargello Museum, Florence
Restored June 2007 – Nov 2008

You were no longer standing there.
Then I saw you lying on your back
propped by wooden slats.
Women worked at you,
scalpelled away the surface grime
in curves and creases of your soft bronze body,
used cautious lasers on Goliath's gilded helmet,
your ornamental boots
your hair and hat.

I was looking down at you, not up to you,
now face to face, neck, hair and shoulders,
eyes on a rounded arm,
five fingers curled against your hip,
the others folded loosely on a hilt –
could you have raised that massive sword?
Eyes move again, caress your soft-hued shining belly,
down to hips and legs angled to catch a girl,
or maybe man?
Not kill a giant.

Your foot is easy on his head,
catching one helmet wing
between your toes
that brush and mingle with his beard,
soft as a dead goat's throat.
The other wing is free,
dead eagle's feather lying against your thigh.

Languid and grave
you contemplate the enemy
under your hat of laurel leaves.
Sensing your gaze
I turn away.

Desert
For Shirley

There is no pity in the sun.
Only my veil gives shadow
to my sleeping child,
only my sweat can moisten him.

Dark, an image keen as flint
I see his head.
The head of Johannan.

Honey Bee
For Michael and Natalie

Suddenly it's warm,
tulip unfurl towards the sun,
the air glitters with beating wings;
a honey bee, legs heavy with flower-feasting
lurches into a single head
and sleeps.

Clouds gather, the tulip closes;
he wakes in a crimson fire
spreading through each petal vein,
kindling the tiny lens and cornea in his compound eyes.
He is cloistered in shot silk, mosaics under shifting water,
the jewelled black and green of stamen pistil.

Lightning Source UK Ltd.
Milton Keynes UK
UKOW04f1738260713

214430UK00001B/9/P